Ethnographic Terminalia: Chicago 2013
Exhibition as Residency—Art, Anthropology, Collaboration
Arts Incubator at Washington Park

© Ethnographic Terminalia, 2014

Published by the Society for Visual Anthropology, a section of the American Anthropological Association. 2300 Clarendon Blvd., Suite 1301. Arlington, VA 22201

Review essays in this volume were originally published in Visual Anthropology Review and SouthSide Weekly. Our grateful acknowledgement to the editors.

Edited by Ethnographic Terminalia:
Craig Campbell, Kate Hennessy, Fiona P. McDonald,
Trudi Lynn Smith, Stephanie Takaragawa

Lead editors and print design: Kate Hennessy, Fiona P. McDonald, and Rachel Topham

Exhibition Photography: Rachel Topham

Cover Design: Ethnographic Terminalia, Rachel Topham and
Ian Kirkpatrick

ISBN 978-1-931303-51-4

Credits   9

Acknowledgements   11

Chicago 2013   13

Ethnographic Terminalia at the Washington Park Arts Incubator   25
Rob Snyder

Artists/Artworks   33

White Walls, "Black City": Reflections on "Exhibition as Residency —   77
Art, Anthropology, Collaboration"
Monique Scott

Sponsors and Supporters   99

Gallery Encounter Posters   100

Chicago 2013:

Contributors

Charlotte Bik Bandlien, *HAiK with us!*   33
and Ruben Steinum

The EBANO Collective   38

Robert Willim   44

Ian Kirkpatrick   50

Jesse Colin Jackson, Tori Foster, and Lindsay A Bell   56

Zoe Bray   62

Joni Olsen, Adam Olsen, Sylvia Olsen, Andrea N. Walsh   68
and Trudi Lynn Smith

Craig Campbell, Kate Hennessy, Fiona P. McDonald,   74
Thomas Ross Miller, Trudi Lynn Smith, Stephanie Takaragawa

Exterior, Arts Incubator, Chicago, 2013

Ethnographic Terminalia

Chicago 2013:

Exhibition as Residency—Art, Anthropology, Collaboration

Arts Incubator in Washington Park

2013 Principal Curator
Fiona P. McDonald

Co-curators
Craig Campbell
Kate Hennessy
Trudi Lynn Smith
Stephanie Takaragawa

Exhibition Photography
Rachel Topham

Graphic Design
Ian Kirkpatrick

SCHOOL OF INTERACTIVE
ARTS + TECHNOLOGY

Acknowledgements

A special thanks to the generosity of our collaborators on the ground in Chicago who really made this effort possible. Thank you to Theaster Gates and his staff at the Arts Incubator in Washington Park for believing in and hosting our efforts in the Project Flex Space. Particular thanks to Allison Glen, J. Alan Love, Norman Teague, Mercedes Sahagun Zavala, and Harold Brown. Also our deepest thanks to the incredible mobilizing efforts in Chicago of Benjamin Haines and the Forest Park Public Library, Elizabeth D'Antonio, and finally to Amavong Panya (NFA Space, Chicago). And to Joanne Smith and her efforts with the Committed Knitters group, as well as Loopy Yarns.

A special mention of gratitude goes to Robert Peterson, Monique Scott, and Roderick Coover to their invaluable and expertise contribution to the roving roundtable discussion at the end of the residency.

We are always grateful for the incredible photographic work of Rachel Topham, and the dynamic design work of Ian Kirkpatrick. Our thanks to Irine Prastio and Reese Muntean for their work on the 2013 website throughout the project. Additionally, we wish to express thanks to Daniel Ruden for acting as the 2013 videographer of the final roundtable event held at the Arts Incubator.

We would like to acknowledge the financial and in-kind support from the American Anthropological Association (Community Engagement Fund), The Society for Visual Anthropology, University of Chicago Art+Public Life Initiative, University College London (Anthropology). University of Texas at Austin (Anthropology), Chapman University (Sociology), and Simon Fraser University (School of Interactive Arts + Technology).

Finally, we would like to express our sincere appreciation to all of the artists who provided documentation for us to include in this project and publication. We would like to thank the artists in Ethnographic Terminalia both for their work and for their participation.

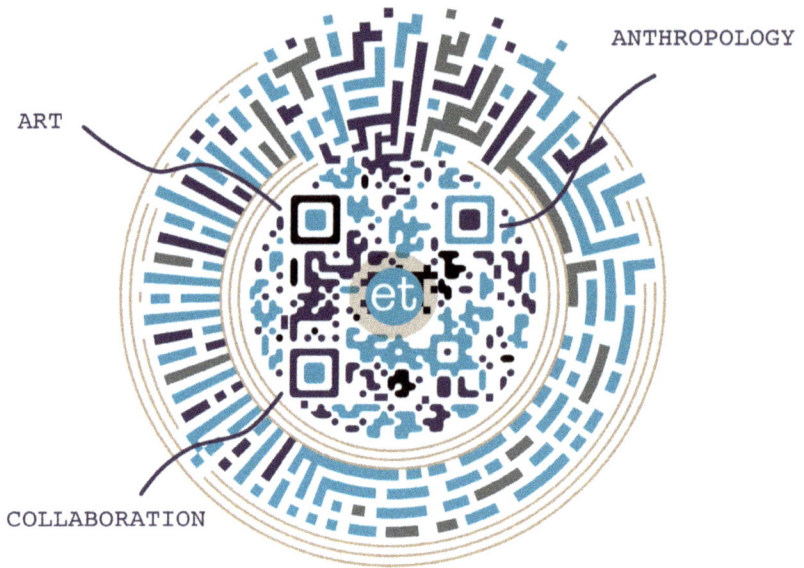

ANTHROPOLOGY

ART

COLLABORATION

et

Chicago 2013:

Exhibition as Residency—Art, Anthropology, Collaboration

Ethnographic Terminalia is an initiative that brings artists and anthropologists together to engage in emerging research through exhibition. *Exhibition as Residency* is an interactive installation of several collaborative projects between artists and anthropologists where visitors are invited to explore what lies within and beyond disciplinary territories of art and anthropology. The performative dimension of this exhibition makes visible how collaborations can shape new communities and innovative representations of cultural practice.

Imagined as an experimental and participatory project, *Exhibition as Residency— Art, Anthropology, Collaboration* draws on both process and collaboration in art and anthropology as central activities and sites of engagement. Over the course of a five-day residency in the Project Flex Space of the Arts Incubator in Washington Park in Chicago, each group of seven projects by artists and anthropologists either produced or developed their distinct ethnographic and/ or artistic research both within the gallery and throughout various sites in Chicago. The 2013 Ethnographic Terminalia project took its inspiration from the framework of the Arts Incubator in Washington Park to become a site of production—an incubator for ideas—where unforeseen cross-pollinations of research and methods can happen between researchers, artists, and local communities. The temporality of the residency offered a passing opportunity for visitors to actively participate in the possibilities of collaboration of knowledge production, or to casually observe how research transpires between artists and anthropologists. The range of artistic and anthropological research on exhibit includes emergent visual research methods for visualizing place, material culture and Indigenous history, film, migration studies, contemporary art, natural/realist painting, fashion design, and curatorial methods.

At its core, Ethnographic Terminalia is experimental and aims at proposing new forms of research and practice, but also finding ground in exhibitions as experimental spaces that provide access to public audiences, new forms of expression for anthropology, and new subjects for artists. In *Exhibition as Residency—Art, Anthropology, Collaboration* we challenged anthropologists and artists to consider new forms of expressing ethnographic details and anthropological theory in process rather than focus on a final product. The result was iterative interactive moments captured through the projects presented here.

Opening reception, Chicago, 2013

Opening reception, Chicago, 2013

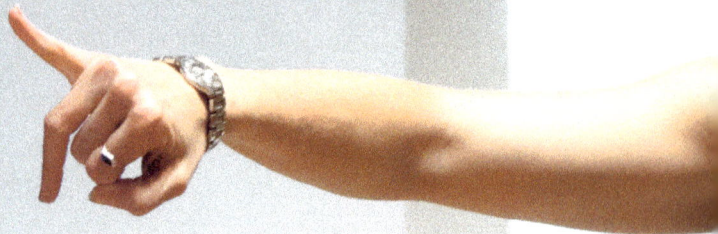

Opening reception, Chicago, 2013

Ian Kirkpatrick discusses his *Habitat*, Chicago, 2013

General installation view, Chicago, 2013

ethnographic terminalia

chicago

2013

exhibition as residency

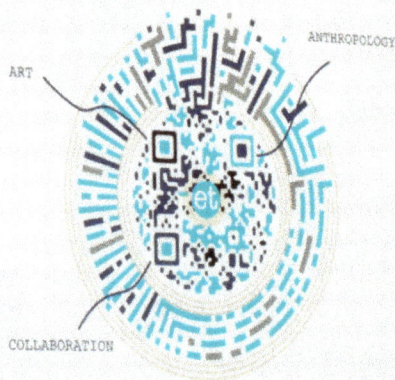

ART
ANTHROPOLOGY
et
COLLABORATION

ETHNOGRAPHIC TERMINALIA
AT THE WASHINGTON PARK ARTS INCUBATOR

Rob Snyder

To hear the artists of Ethnographic Terminalia tell it, the discipline of anthropology is in a state of crisis. In the 1980s, "people started to talk about what you lose when you write about culture," says Charlotte Bik Bandlien, which prompted a critique of the staid confines of academia. Ethnographic Terminalia offers an alternative way to study culture: through art. It purports to be art not just inspired by human beings and human culture, but art that can be seen as equal in rigor to traditional forms of anthropological analysis— hence the title of Ethnographic Terminalia's exhibit at the Washington Park Arts Incubator, "Exhibition as Residency." The question that this exhibit raises has radical implications: Why does academia, with its stuffy conferences and formal papers, hold dominance over research and intellectual thought?

Every artist whose work was displayed at Ethnographic Terminalia is a trained anthropologist seeking to break down disciplinary boundaries. Other than that vision, there isn't much else that this uneven collective has in common. Drawn from around the globe, each artist presents a unique way in which art can conduct ethnographies and express the core tenet of anthropology—the study of human beings and culture—in new ways and to new audiences.

Zoe Bray, a trained painter and an anthropologist at the University of Nevada's Reno campus, displayed three portraits at the exhibition. Her involvement with

Reprinted with permission. Snyder, Rob. 2013. Exhibition Review. ART-THROPOLOGY: Ethnographic Terminalia at the Washington Park Arts Incubator. Southside Weekly. Available at: http://southsideweekly.com/art-thropology/#more-1180

Facing page, title wall, *Exhibition as Residency,* Chicago, 2013

Artist and Anthrologist Zoe Bray with model, Chicago, 2013

Ethnographic Terminalia came about due to what she calls her "frustration with rigid academia" and a desire to "break out of the mold." However, her new approach is not rebellion for its own sake. Bray says her relationship with her portrait models was far richer and more natural than an anthropologist's usual rapport with a subject, because people simply opened up to an artist more than an anthropologist's open-ended, scientific, objectifying questions.

The EBANO Collective, based out of Portugal, sees art as a way to broaden the audience of anthropological research. "Work is usually site-specific, so we bring it inside the gallery" says Vitor Barros. In doing so, EBANO Collective questions what constitutes a legitimate space of expression. As anthropologists, they study the vexing paradox of migration: new opportunity coupled with the dangers of moving. Their piece is a tall wooden bookshelf-like structure with white heads sitting in water-filled jars on the shelves, like something out of a mad scientist's laboratory. The higher shelves have heads directly on the shelf, sans jar, and perched at the top is the flag of the European Union. Barros explains that the artwork evokes the memory of immigrants who die in the

Facing page, EBANO's *Shrines of Citizenship*, Chicago, 2013

Mediterranean Sea, whose hopes for opportunity were cut short by the perils of migration.

Charlotte Bik Bandlien sees her work as the natural extension of art incorporating anthropology, rather than the other way around. Her piece is "HAiK," a fashion catalog featuring self-repair clothing items, or clothes that are meant to be continuously repaired by the individual and maintained for life. Engaging with the fashion design process is another way of analyzing anthropological material, she says, a way of recognizing that moments of ethnography exist beyond interviews and emerge naturally in social processes, like photographing a model. If it were anywhere outside of an anthropology-inspired art gallery, it would be an ordinary fashion catalog. In the context of this exhibit, Bandlien deliberately mimics the form of a catalog in order to question what constitutes ethnography.

The result of these and other artistic visions of anthropology is a wild conglomeration of ideas. To judge the exhibit on whether it achieves a seismic shift in an academic discipline is unfair; the exhibit sets out to express new ideas and challenge accepted notions, which it succeeds in doing.

But freeing ethnography from the insulated sphere of academic conferences raises new issues. An academic paper has a clear audience and sphere for discussion, but who is the target of an academic art exhibit? If the artists of Ethnographic Terminalia wish to make good on their hopes of expanding the audience of anthropology, they must make a concerted effort in doing so with the way their art is expressed.

Facing page, Charlotte Bik Bandlien and Ruben Steinum's *Self Repair* Chicago, 2013

Roundtable discussion, Chicago, 2013

Charlotte Bik Bandlien and Ruben Steinum's *Self Repair* Chicago, 2013

Charlotte Bik Bandlien
HAiK with us!
Ruben Steinum
Self-Repair
mixed media
2013

Integrating critical discourses of art, anthropology and fashion, this team explores the notion of "self-repair". The project is an extension of a residency in Norway at the Rogaland Art Center that investigated the notion of repair in terms of the relationship between the industrial manufactured and touch of hands with needle and thread. For Chicago, this collective expanded the notion of repair to research the topic of "self-repair" (ex. self-help, life coaching, positive thinking, aura-reading etc.). In line with the experimental ambition of the residency in the Arts Incubator, their research in Chicago explored similarities between anthropological and artistic methods in terms of participant observation and subjective interpretations. During the residency they developed a new pattern for a textile inspired and informed by this research specific to Chicago. The pattern was further developed after the residency, and the research from Chicago formed the basis for a Chicago-line within the HAiK collection for 2015 (released in late-2014).

Websites:
http://cbb.no/index.php?/about/
http://www.haikwithus.com/?page_id=150
http://rubensteinum.com

This project is funded in part by OCA—Office for Contemporary Art Norway

Charlotte Bik Bandlien (Norway) is an Oslo-based anthropologist specializing in material and visual culture. She is an Assistant Professor and course Director at the Oslo National Academy of the Arts in the Department of Design (since 2011), and a contributing editor to the Norwegian fashion journal, Personae.

Ida Falck Øien (Norway) is an Oslo-based artist with a background in fine art and design. She is cofounder of the clothing label and collaborative platform HAiK with us! (since 2011) and is currently working on a commission for the Odontological (Medical) Faculty of the University of Bergen to create uniforms.

Ruben Steinum (Norway) is an artist who lives and works in Oslo. He received his BFA from the Oslo National Academy of the Arts and is currently the Deputy Chair at the Young Artists Society. Recently he launched the publication Casual Maneuver—A Step Away from It at the exhibition spaces Entreé and Kunsthall Oslo.

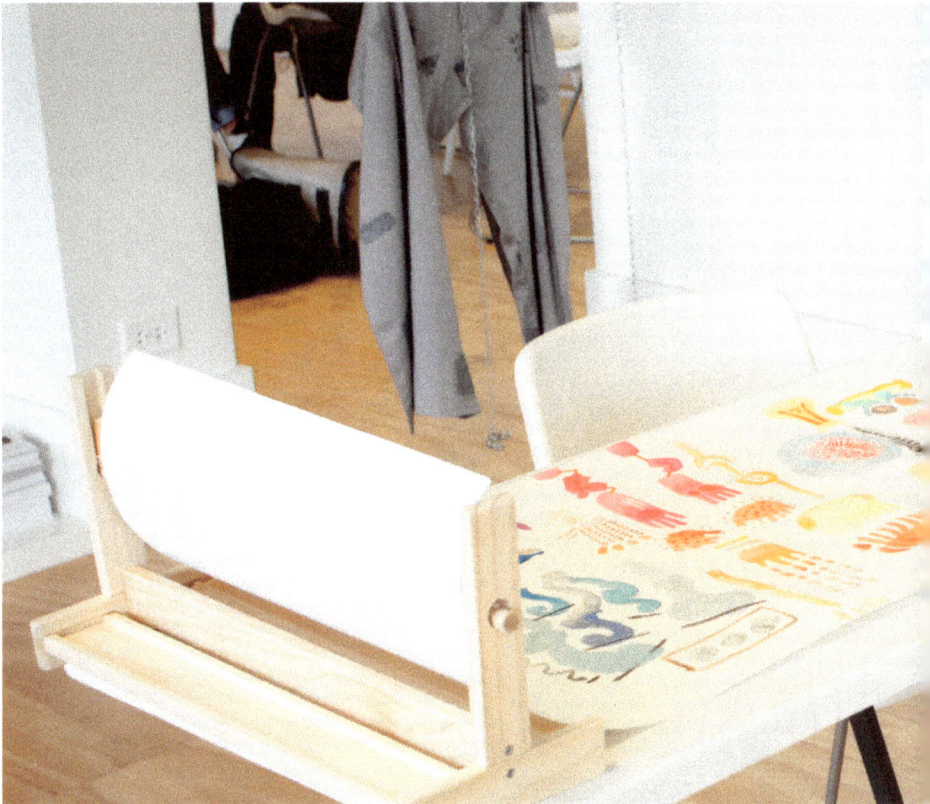

SHRINES OF CITIZENSHIP

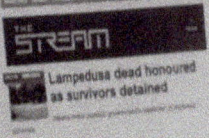

SHRINES OF CITIZENSHIP

THE STREAM

Lampedusa dead honoured as survivors detained

ALJA

EBANO Collective
Lorenzo Bordonaro
Chiara Pussetti
Vitor Barros
Shrines of Citizenship
wood, glass, water, wax, sand, fabric, paper, LED lights
2013

The EBANO Collective uses diverse art forms and media to explore the imaginaries ascribed to migration. Based upon several years of anthropological fieldwork with immigrant communities in Europe, their multimedia installation *Shrines of Citizenship* invited visitors to reflect upon the recent tightening of European migration policies, as well as the physical, bureaucratic, and symbolic barriers undocumented immigrants around the world face when pursuing the dream of citizenship. Water, wax, and other devotional objects, such as an encased passport, allude to the complexity of mobility and citizenship along all national borders, specifically evoking the memory of the thousands of people that in the last decades disappeared in the Mediterranean sea attempting to reach Europe's southern border.

Websites:
http://www.ebanocollective.org/
www.woundscapes.com

This project is funded by the EBANO Collective and the Calouste Gulbenkian Foundation

Lorenzo Bordonaro (Portugal) is the president of the EBANO Collective. As an anthropologist and artist he has conducted research on youth, childhood, creativity, and urban marginality in Guinea Bissau (since 1996), Cape Verde (since 2007), and Lisbon. He is currently exploring the intersections between public art, ethnography, and urban intervention.

Chiara Pussetti (Portugal) is an anthropologist who has published extensively on the subjects of the anthropology of body and emotions, medical anthropology, and migration studies. She is a member of the EBANO Collective. Her extensive fieldwork looks at mental health and emotions in Guinea Bissau and Portugal.

Vitor Barros (UK) is a PhD candidate at King's College London (UK) and a researcher in the areas of history of medicine, public health, and the social care sector. He is also an independent photographer and multimedia producer. Together with fellow EBANO Collective member Chiara Pussetti he curated the exhibition Woundscapes in Brazil.

Robert Willim
Imaginary Venues [Almost There—Washington Park]
film
2013

Imaginary Venues [Almost There—Washington Park] –an original
experimental film that presents a surreal account of imagined venues
associated with Washington Park area in Chicago. Produced over the
course of the residency, the film gathers together imagery and factual
material associated with the City of Chicago's bid to host the 2016
Olympic Summer Games, in which Washington Park was proposed as
the main site for the Olympic arena. While Chicago lost the bid to Rio
de Janeiro, the 'dream' to host the games is now part of the city's history.
As an artist and anthropologist, Willim built upon a larger project,
Fieldnotes, to understand the extent to which dreamscapes associated
with place can enchant a city.

website:
http://robertwillim.com/

This project is funded in part by Lund University

Robert Willim (Sweden), an artist and anthropologist (ethnologist), is an Associate Professor at Lund University in Sweden. His art is positioned in the borderland next to his academic practices as a cultural analyst and ethnographer. He uses his research to spur artistic concepts and to explore the interplay between representation and evocation, as well as art and anthropology.

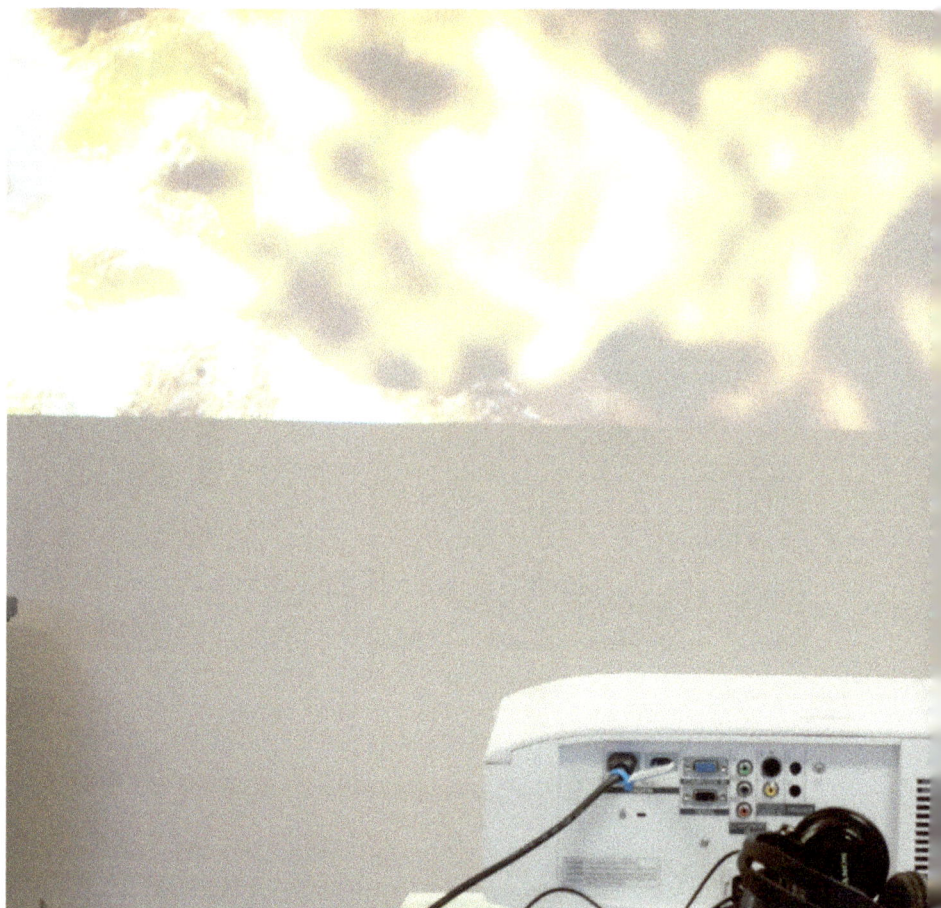

Ian Kirkpatrick
Habitat
cardboard, ink, paint, pencil
2013

This sculptural installation invited visitors to observe artistic practice in situ within a temporary, makeshift studio. Ian Kirkpatrick will create his own 'habitat' out of cardboard, inspired by consumer packaging as well as ancient containers such as Greek amphorae and Egyptian sarcophagi. The artist inhabited the sculptural work during the residency, illuminating it from within with iconography informed via observations within the gallery, research at local museums, and impressions of Chicago at large. This performative installation highlighted the engagement of artists with museum anthropology in the creation of new cultural forms.

website:
http://iankirkpatrick.wordpress.com/

Ian Kirkpatrick (UK-based) is a Canadian contemporary artist and graphic designer currently based in the UK. His fine art has been exhibited internationally since 2008, including recent shows in London, New York, and Berlin.

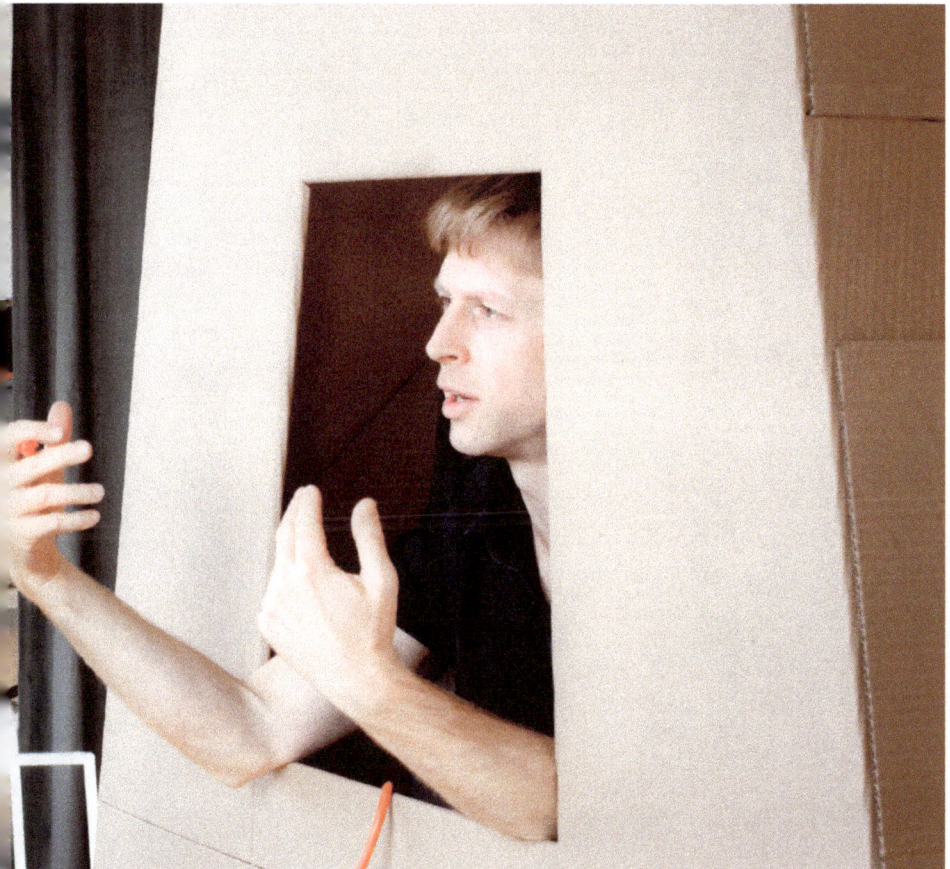

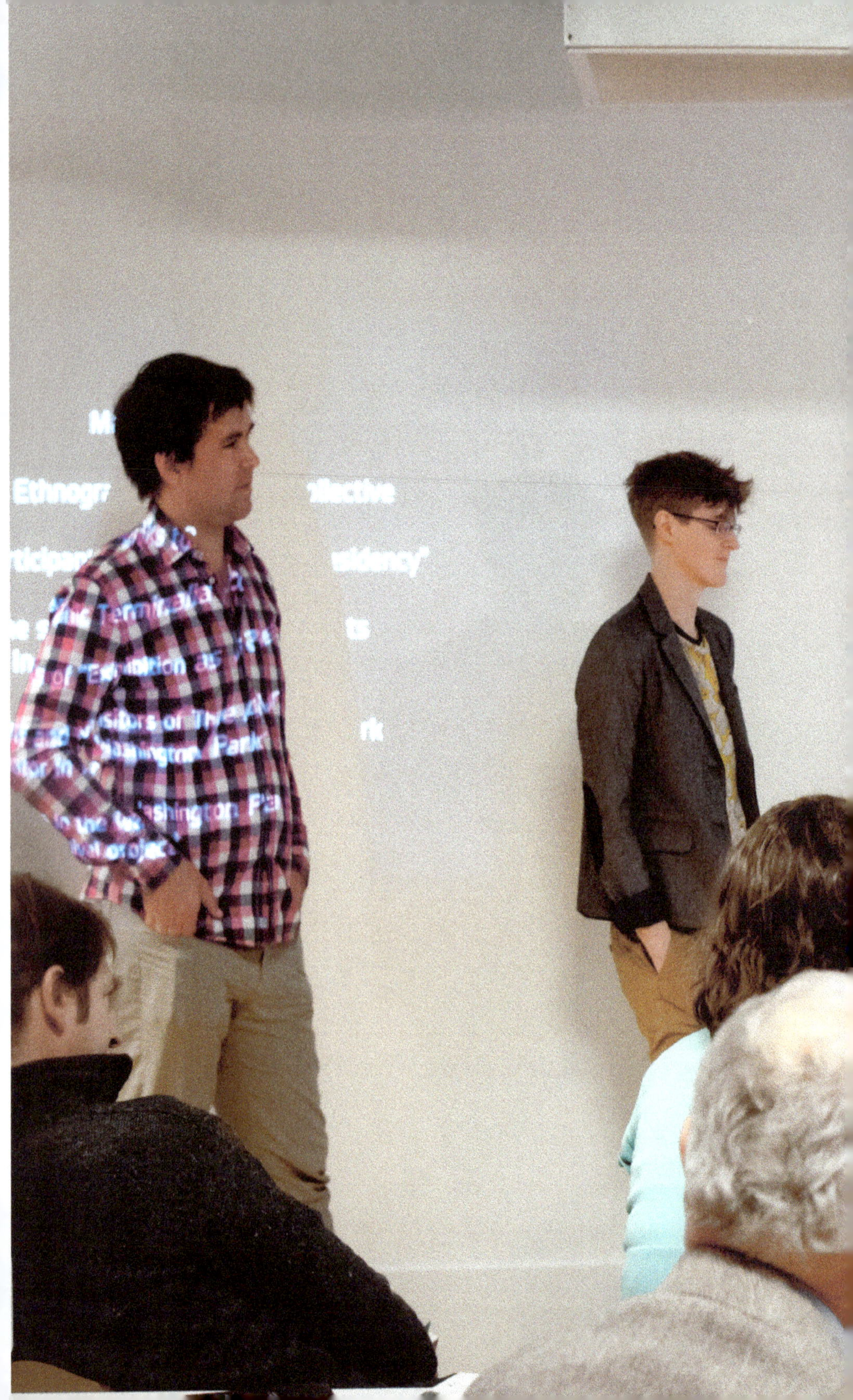

Visualizing Canada's Urban North
Lindsay A Bell
Tori Foster
Jesse Jackson
Visualizing Arts and Public Life
photographs, video
2013

Visualizing Arts and Public Life provided an opportunity for the Visualizing Canada's Urban North research team to refine and experiment with their strategies for translating urban information into visual form. Their site-specific project at the residency allowed them to test their research methods through short-term observation and subsequent visual recombination of the territory in and around Chicago's Arts Incubator. Engagement with gallery visitors will facilitate rapid methodological evolution, culminating in the presentation of work-in-progress composite photos and video.

websites:
http://utoronto.academia.edu/LindsayABell
http://www.torifoster.com/
http://www.jessecolinjackson.com/
http://www.civ-ddd.net/project/urban-information-and-representation-initiative/

This project is funded in part by the Social Sciences and Humanities Research Council of Canada, and the Centre for Information Visualization and Data Driven Design established by the Ontario Research Fund.

Lindsay A. Bell (Canada) is a SSHRC funded Faculty Associate in Women and Gender Studies at the University of Toronto. Specializing in the industrial development and urbanization of Circumpolar North America, her research and writing strives to understand how northern populations shape and relate to large-scale social, environmental and economic change.

Tori Foster (Canada) is a Toronto-based media artist whose work centers upon emergent behavior and the urban landscape. Her works are heavily process oriented, exposing information inherent to, but not visible in, unmediated environments. She is currently Adjunct Professor in Research and Graduate Studies at OCAD University.

Jesse Colin Jackson (USA) is a Los Angeles based artist and designer whose work appropriates and recontextualizes the images, forms, and conceptual apparatus found in the urban landscape. He was educated as an architect and engineer, and is currently an Assistant Professor of Art at the University of California, Irvine.

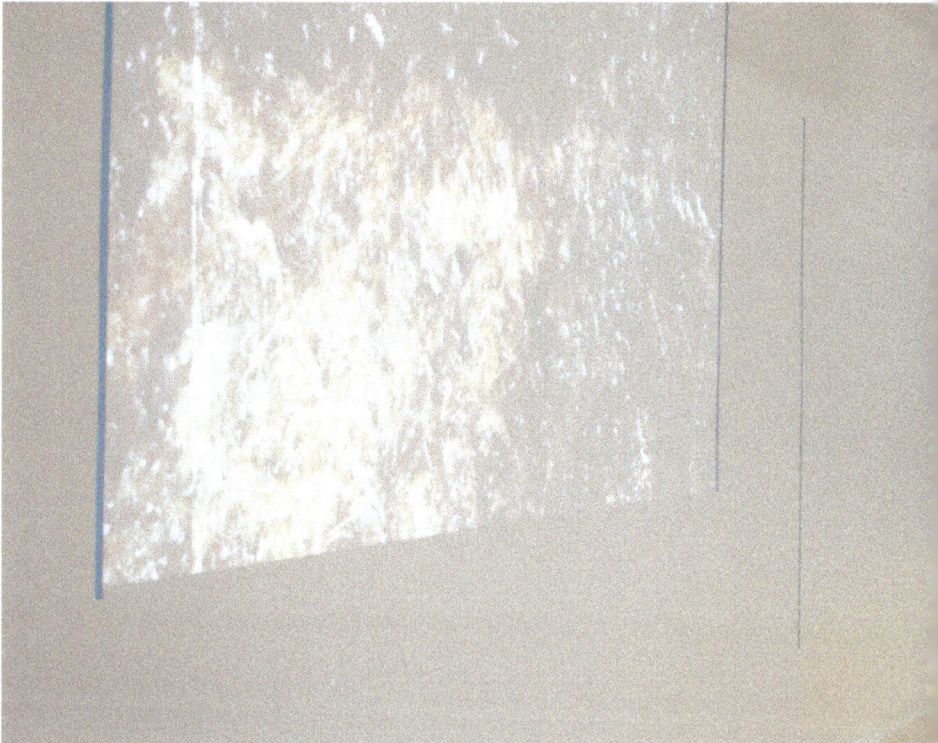

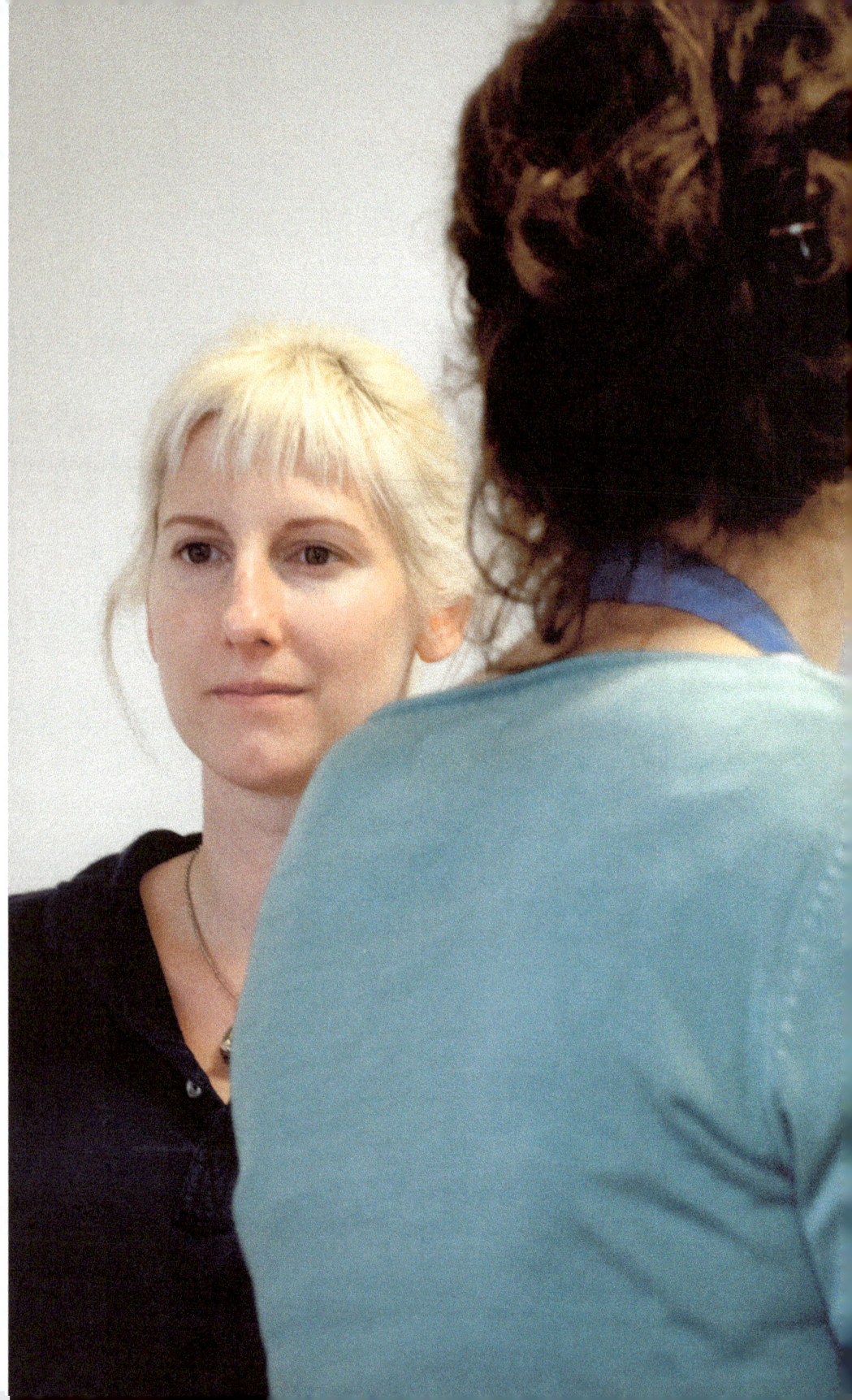

Zoe Bray
The Ethnographic Process of Portrait-Painting

2013

During the residency, Zoe Bray live-painted within the gallery space
to explore further her methodological connections between naturalist
(also know as realist) painting and ethnography. By demonstrating
ethnographic research methods such as cultural immersion, participant-
observation, open-ended interviews, and reflective selection, Bray draws
parallels to techniques employed in naturalist painting such as the use
of the mirror, squinting, distance, and choice of focus. This project is an
ongoing effort that explores at an epistemological level how painting
and ethnography share a common concern with apprehension of
the objective world by means long-term observation and contextual
interaction.

websites:
http://www.zoebray.net/Zoe_Bray/Bio.html
http://basque.unr.edu/academics-people-bray.html

This project is funded in part by the University of Nevada, Reno and the
Center for Basque Studies

Zoe Bray (UK/Basque Country) is a realist painter and social anthropologist. Since 2011, she has been an Assistant Professor in the Center for Basque Studies in Anthropology and Art at the University of Nevada, Reno. Her current research on 'The Artist as Hero: Art and Politics in the Basque Country Today' uses portrait painting as an additional ethnographic method in her fieldwork.

Current and facing page, Zoe Bray painting a portrait of visual anthropologist Dr. Thomas Blakely, Chicago, 2013

Joni Olsen
Adam Olsen
Sylvia Olsen
Andrea N. Walsh
Trudi Lynn Smith
Re-connections: Coast Salish Knitting and Resilience in Chicago
wool and video
2013

Re-connections began as a conversation between Coast Salish knitters, anthropologists, artists, and a historian, about the tensions between academic knowledge production and creative practices in Indigenous communities. The group was interested in re-connecting contemporary Coast Salish knitters from the northwest coast of Canada with Coast Salish woven wool artifacts, collected in the late 19th century for exhibition at the 1893 Columbia World's Fair, now part of the collection of the Chicago Field Museum. The primary purpose of the creative research was to provide contemporary knitters an opportunity to research the historical wool artifacts and the history of their collection in the colonial archive. The knitters fused this experience of working with their practice of designing and producing contemporary wool garments and produced a new garment in the gallery. The group also filmed a ceremonial blanket performance at a replica of the 1893 World's Fair monument, entitled *A Signal for Peace* (C. Dalin) and after the ceremony, the blanket, produced on Tsartlip First Nation territory just outside Victoria, B.C. was gifted and accessioned into the Field Museum contemporary collection of northwest coast art, creating a material re-connection between the historical wool artifacts in the collection, their makers, and the contemporary Salish knitters, and their own cultural production.

websites:
http://anthropology.uvic.ca/people/faculty/walsh.php
http://salishfusion.ca/coast-salish-sharing-their-traditions-at-uvic/

This project funded in part by First Peoples' Heritage, Language & Culture Council

Adam Olsen (Coast Salish from the Tsartlip First Nation near Victoria, BC, Canada) is a proficient machine knitter. He designs knitted fabric that he transforms into innovative wearable and household products. He is co-owner of Salish Fusion with his sister, Joni, and mother, Sylvia.

Joni Olsen (Coast Salish from the Tsartlip First Nation near Victoria, BC, Canada) is a hand and machine knitter who learned the art of making Cowichan Sweaters that she fuses with new knitting techniques and designs to make projects for her company, Salish Fusion, that she co-owns with her brother, Adam, and mother, Sylvia.

Sylvia Olsen (Canada) has a long history in First Nations wool working on Southern Vancouver Island. She studied the rich history of Cowichan Salish knitters for her master's thesis after having moved to the Tsartlip First Nation with her Coast Salish husband. She started the Olsen family Cowichan sweater business, Salish Fusion, and is the author of many historical fiction books for young people.

Andrea Walsh (Canada), a visual anthropologist and artist, is an Associate Professor at the University of Victoria. Her research with contemporary Indigenous artists focuses on art as a method of communicating Indigenous experiences of history and identity. She is Canadian with Irish, British, Scottish, Nlaka'pamux, and Sxw'whámel ancestry.

Trudi Lynn Smith (Canada) is an artist and visual anthropologist who studies practices of photography. She currently holds a position at York University as a SSHRC Post Doctoral Fellow in the Department of Humanities. In writing, artworks, and performances, she explores the photograph as event, following fleeting moments and shifting visualities in archives and on the ground.

Craig Campbell
Kate Hennessy
Fiona P. McDonald
Thomas Ross Miller
Trudi Lynn Smith
Stephanie Takaragawa
Ethnographic Terminalia Curatorial Collective
2013

The curators of Ethnographic Terminalia acted in two capacities over the week of the Residency. First, they worked with fellow Residents to articulate possibilities associated with exhibition and public engagement for collaborating artists and anthropologists. Second, members of the collective took the opportunity to reflect upon their first five years of collaborative experimentation with the intersections of anthropology and art from New York (2013), San Francisco (2012), Montreal (2011), New Orleans (2010), and Philadelphia (2009)

websites:
www.ethnographicterminalia.org
https://www.facebook.com/groups/terminalia

ethnographic terminalia
chicago
2013

exhibition as residency

WHITE WALLS, "BLACK CITY":

REFLECTIONS ON

"EXHIBITION AS RESIDENCY—ART, ANTHROPOLOGY, COLLABORATION"

Monique Scott PhD.

There is a common perception, perhaps misperception, that High Art exists in white spaces—aesthetically clean white gallery spaces populated by prestigious white cultural producers and consumers of a similar ilk. The signifying potency of whiteness in exhibition spaces persists in the popular imagination and finds an unyielding legacy in exhibition history. At the 1893 World's Fair held in Chicago, the famed "White City" referred to the exposition's "Court of Honor"—a set of illuminated white stucco buildings created to construct a sterilized image of Chicagoan beauty as a conscious counter to the darker slums and tenements that tainted the image of the city in the nineteenth century. This re-branding of Chicago was provocatively suggestive of purity in aesthetics and culture and also served as a civilizing ritual. This type of institutional white-washing resonates with many present-day high art galleries, which too often cultivate a sense of cultural ascension and create borders between themselves and their audiences. Yet some galleries also strive to move away from the stigma of whiteness and creatively work to diversify their image, their audiences, and their cultural producers.

An extraordinary example of the departure from hierarchical exhibition conventions is the pioneering gallery known as the Arts Incubator in Washington Park located in Garfield in South Chicago, recent home of the exhibition: *Exhibition as Residency—Art, Anthropology, Collaboration* from November 18th-22nd, 2013, organized by the progressive international curatorial collective, Ethnographic Terminalia. By curating works at the intersection of art and anthropology, the Collective takes anthropology outside

Reprinted with permission. Monique Scott. 2014. Exhibition Review Essay. "White Walls, 'Black City': Reflections on 'Exhibition as Residency—Art, Anthropology, Collaboration'." Visual Anthropology Review 30 (2): 190-198.

Exterior, Arts Incubator, Chicago, 2013

Exhibition as Residency, Chicago, 2013

of the narrow confines of academia to create novel, contemporary sites of public anthropological engagement. Ethnographic Terminalia is composed of six anthropologists and artists including Craig Campbell, Kate Hennessy, Fiona P. McDonald, Thomas Ross Miller, Trudi Lynn Smith, and Stephanie Takaragawa. The Collective has curated four previous exhibitions since 2009, each in conjunction with the American Anthropological Association (AAA) conferences in Philadelphia, New Orleans, Montréal, and San Francisco. According to Fiona P. McDonald, anthropologist and curator from the Ethnographic Terminalia collective for the 2013 exhibition, "This year in Chicago we set out to create conversations with and within Chicago by taking up residency at the Arts Incubator in hopes of participating in and bringing international responses to local conversations."

For *Exhibition as Residency,* Ethnographic Terminalia broke new ground by collaborating with the Southside's acclaimed Arts Incubator of the University of Chicago's Arts + Public Life Initiative to install in their Project Flex Space on the second level of the Incubator. The Arts Incubator in Washington Park encourages cultural renewal in South Chicago by bringing a "high art" gallery to an economically depressed neighborhood in order to create a space where the community can come together to collaboratively produce and appreciate art. It is under the directorship of the internationally famed artist Theaster Gates. In a January 20th, 2014 New Yorker article entitled, "The Real-Estate Artist: High-concept renewal on the South Side," Jeffrey Deitch (the former director of the Museum of Contemporary art in LA) shares about Gates, "His special fusion of art and community activism has made him the kind of artist that people are looking for today. It's not just addressing issues of art about art, and art about self-identity; it's a new vocabulary, a new approach. The success of his work is measured by its actual impact on the community." According to McDonald, "Theaster Gates, to whom we are grateful for his openness in seeing potential for a conversation between anthropologists and the community around the Arts Incubator. On the meta-level of undertaking a residency, Ethnographic Terminalia was initially creating a response to the exciting framework that the Arts Incubator has established since its opening in March 2013, just eight months prior to our exhibition, and we were consciously embracing the work that Theaster Gates performs both in the Arts Incubator but also in his larger art practice." A goal of *Exhibition as Residency* was to integrate, to take residency, among the culture of the neighborhood, rather that assume the distance conventionally taken up by artists closed off in gallery spaces. Furthermore, while it was not necessarily the main focus of the exhibition, by installing *Exhibition as Residency* in the Arts Incubator, it did, however, create a space to reflect upon the dialectics of race and class that transpire when predominately white artists take up residency in a predominately Black South Chicago neighborhood.

My response in this exhibition review stems not only from my time of visiting the gallery, but also from my experience as a discussant for the closing roundtable conversation about the exhibition on its last day at the Arts Incubator. This culminating event brought together the artists, the Ethnographic Terminalia curators, and two other outside discussants, Robert Peterson (NYC-based artist and curator) and Roderick Coover (Professor of Film and Media Arts at Temple University, Philadelphia) who themselves had exhibited in past Ethnographic Terminalia exhibitions (Coover-2009 and Peterson-2010). The roundtable provided an important glimpse into the artists' motivations, processes, and reflections that I present throughout the rest of this review and that I contextualize in relation to my own observations.

In *Exhibition as Residency,* Ethnographic Terminalia curated works that were globally, aesthetically, and conceptually diverse from seven different groups comprised of artists and anthropologists who carried out their research in residence for five days in South Chicago—a territory that I assume was somewhat alien to them—in order to engage their anthropological and artistic research methods with new audiences and communities. During the week, exhibitors were invited to experiment with their collaborative research practices and share with each other and with visitors the opportunity to create responsive, reflective works that merge methodologies, media, topics, and themes. Over the five days of the residency, Ethnographic Terminalia also broke ground in curating an exhibition that refreshingly focused almost as much on process as product and put the artists themselves on display as objects under the outsider's gaze.

With *Exhibition as Residency,* this inspired collection of artists and anthropologists took up the challenging and elusive question of how artists truly inhabit and engage novel spaces around them. That primarily anthropologists undertook this ambitious project makes the larger exhibition even more nuanced as it created another space for dialogue around not only art but anthropology as well. Coinciding with the 112th American Anthropological Association (AAA) meetings happening simultaneously in downtown Chicago, this exhibition represented a public face of anthropology. Anthropologists often wrestle with themes of identity and place, being insiders and outsiders, with intimacy and alienation, and with the overarching challenge of creating meaningful relationships and thick interpretations of an-other culture. And during this weighty process, anthropologists have increasingly become self-reflexive in the visual presentation of their research—a reflexivity that this exhibition addressed in creative and critical ways.

The marriage of Ethnographic Terminalia and the Arts Incubator was ripe for harmonic and disharmonic convergences that offer unique academic and artistic insights. However, while the richness of the artistic products was unquestionable, it is quite challenging to evaluate the overall impact of the residency—an entanglement of experiences, expectations, and outcomes. And of course, what we glean from this exhibition as outsiders is also relative to our own biased perspectives. For me, this was admittedly about being a female Black anthropologist who studies museum audiences and not gallery art, and was thus intimidated in my own way by the predominately white atmosphere in the *Exhibition as Residency* gallery space. Yet this outsider-ness in the exhibition space was also complicated by being equally disconnected from the external atmosphere. I, too, was entering the neighborhood of the Arts Incubator and the exhibition for only a few days, a few ephemeral experiences. My own research has given me a healthy respect and cynicism at an outsider's ability to evaluate process. Given the complex constellation of influences that determine how meaning is made in exhibitions, the greater cultural matrix in which exhibitions and their visitors are situated constitutes a site where anthropological knowledge becomes co-produced on multiple levels between makers, curators, institutions, and audiences. From my vantage point, co-production was certainly inherent to *Exhibition as Residency*—where new meanings were continually being produced, evolving, and responding to the interplay of artists and audiences.

Artists, Artworks, and Audience

In keeping with their goals, Ethnographic Terminalia set up a number of participatory audience events throughout the week of the residency to facilitate the convergence of artist, artwork, and the local community. The exhibition was open daily from 12 to 3pm for the public to see and ask questions about the projects under construction. Although the exhibition did not reach the level of visitation it sought from the local community, the investment in public engagement was evident in the intention. And in some moments, the intention was more than met, as when the Coast Salish knitting workshop clearly succeeded in engaging the community

As I mentioned, innumerable connections can be made between the artworks and projects produced for *Exhibition as Residency* when we think of the co-production of knowledge. In the nexus of artists and anthropologists that converged on the Arts Incubator space, three distinct connections were very apparent to me. I use these thematic organizations to organize my discussion of the works in the exhibition: (1) those that emphasize how we see and exhibit culture; (2) those that represent certain profound aesthetic innovations; and (3) those that aimed at true cultural immersions.

Exhibiting Culture

Ian Kirkpatrick and Zoe Bray placed both themselves and their artistic endeavors on display. Their forward approach to exhibiting visual research methods such as painting and drawing allowed visitors to question how intimacy arises between artist and artwork, and to meditate on artistic process in rich ways. It also illuminated the shifting role of insiders and outsiders to a work of art and the process of producing art.

In the work of artist and graphic designer Ian Kirkpatrick, *Habitat* (UK), Kirkpatrick provoked viewers to think about how we look: This sculptural installation invited visitors to observe artistic practice in situ within a temporary, makeshift studio. Ian Kirkpatrick created his own "habitat" out of cardboard, inspired by consumer packaging as well as ancient containers such as Greek amphorae and Egyptian sarcophagi. The artist inhabited the work during the residency, illuminating the sculptural object from within with iconography

Ian Kirkpatrick, *Habitat*, Chicago, 2013

informed via observations within the gallery, research at local museums, and impressions of Chicago at large. This performative installation highlights the engagement of artists with the historic conventions of museum anthropology in the creation of new cultural forms (ET2013 Gallery Guide).

Kirkpatrick's work evoked the 1893 Chicago Exposition, as well as other large-scale public exhibitions; by putting himself on display, his installation became a living reflection on exhibiting others, challenging the history of othering by placing himself, the white, male artist, on display as an object of anthropological knowledge. Due to the lack of attendance by the local community, however, the juxtaposition of power positions could not become fully realized because he was mostly an artist on display to his peers rather than on display for the local community. Interestingly, Kirkpatrick also noted the instability of his work. In process and "without an endpoint," *Habitat* was not an installation that most art galleries would exhibit; rather, it was a site-specific response to the Project Flex Space within the Arts Incubator.

Likewise, anthropologist Zoe Bray's *The Ethnographic Process of Portrait Painting* (UK/Basque Country) put on display her practices of painting as an ethnographic method of qualitative data collection. Through painting her models while conducting field interviews, she produces a progressive form of ethnography that creates new ways of thinking about how anthropologists engage their subjects. Like Kirkpatrick's *Habitat*, Bray's work reflects on process, extending to the destruction, and not simply construction, of her paintings: During the Residency, Zoe Bray live-painted in the gallery space to explore further her methodological connections between naturalist (also know as realist) painting and ethnography. By demonstrating ethnographic research methods such as cultural immersion, participant-observation, open-ended interviews, and reflective selection, Bray draws parallels between ways of looking. For example, through her work she connects the techniques employed in naturalist painting such as the use of the mirror, squinting, distance, and choice of focus, to the intense participant observation anthropologists are often trained to use during their fieldwork. At an epistemological level this installation explored how painting and ethnography share a common concern with apprehension of the objective world by means of long-term observation and contextual interaction (ET2013 Gallery Guide).

Facing page, Zoe Bray, Chicago, 2013

Eager to engage in dialogue with visitors during her painting process, Bray established an active rather than passive exhibition space. Bray stopped painting her model, Dr. Tom Blakely, a well-regarded visual anthropologist, every 20 minutes to discuss her unique ethnographic process with her audience. Reflecting on her experience in Chicago, Bray mentioned that she was disappointed more visitors, particularly young people, were not present for daily exchanges. Improvising (a strength of several of these artists), she inserted herself into the Coast Salish knitting workshop that took place in the gallery by setting herself and her model within proximity of the public workshop. This arrangement created a striking visual and conceptual immersion. In addition, Bray's work at the Arts Incubator departed from her primary research focus on Basque communities overseas. When undertaking her painting in the gallery space, she put anthropologists as models for her paintings on display. This created a challenging new meta-level layer of interpretation and deepened the experience of having anthropology on display—a clear goal of Ethnographic Terminalia as a collective.

Aesthetic Innovations

Two projects featured in *Exhibition as Residency* focused on film and digital imaging to make aesthetic interventions into how we think of and see space, as well as the shifting cultures that inhabit a place—first, *Visualizing Arts and Public Life* by anthropologist Lindsay Bell, and artists Tori Foster and Jesse Colin Jackson, and second *Almost There: Imaginary Venues* by artist/anthropologist Robert Willim. The avant-garde methodologies in film and digital media challenged audiences to re-think ways of seeing and visualizing landscapes around the Arts Incubator.

With *Visualizing Arts and Public Life* (USA/Canada), the Visualizing Canada's Urban North team created several works that interrogated the possibilities for reading the intersection of art and anthropology and how we perceive the instability of urban spaces: the work provided an opportunity for the research team to refine their collaborative strategies for translating urban information into visual form. Their site-specific project at the residency allowed them to test their research methods through short-term observation and subsequent visual recombination of the territory in and around the Washington Park area (ET2013 Gallery Guide).

By installing cameras that looked within and outside of the gallery, the team collected data that was sliced together to create a sense of time, activity, and place. Looking at their photo and film documentation while visiting the gallery, we see layer upon layer of meaning mutate as the artists use translucent overlays and other technologies to recreate landscape. The moving layers of images, however, are all "real" and in some ways are themselves a form of data visualization. Bell and Foster also reflected upon their process during the closing roundtable when they shared the limited amount of time they spent in the environment collecting footage versus the many hours they spent intensely focused on the production of the work. They were able to acknowledge the critical nature of time to their research methods and that perhaps these methods didn't suit the notion of residency after all—an honest reflection that created an insight into both the time artists spent looking outside (at the world) and looking "inside," entrenched in the production of their work.

In *Imaginary Venues [Almost There—Washington Park]* (Sweden), Robert Willim created an experimental film that presents a surreal account of imagined venues associated with the Washington Park area in Chicago. Produced over the course of the residency, the film gathered imagery and factual material associated with the city of Chicago's bid to host the 2016 Olympic Summer Games, in which Washington Park was proposed as the main site for the Olympic arena. While Chicago lost the bid to Rio de Janeiro, the "dream" of hosting the games is now part of the city's history. As an artist and anthropologist, this project in Chicago builds upon *Fieldnotes*, a larger project where Willim attempts to understand the extent to which dreamscapes associated with place can enchant a city (from the Exhibition Brochure).

Robert Willim's film mixed the real and the imagined, producing an imaginative geography with important political and cultural implications for how we understand both Washington Park and Chicago at large. It provocatively refers back to the Columbian Exposition by considering Chicago as a hopeful host to an international spectacle that would have put the city on display in a contemporary context through sport. As he filmed his footage of the Washington Park area, Willim felt "intentionally ambivalent" about this work as residency, admitting that the stories he constructs are site-specific mediations that can be produced without even visiting the environment—a compelling challenge in and of itself to the notion of residency.

Cultural Immersions

Three other contributions to *Exhibition as Residency* capture the art of cultural immersion. Three works, (1) *Self-Repair;* (2) *Shrines of Citizenship;* and (3) and *Re-connections: Coast Salish Knitting and Resilience in Chicago,* examined residency in immediate ways by creating works that explicitly embodied the cultures of Chicago. Often these artists and anthropologists attempted to immerse themselves in the city's communities and, in doing so, occasionally provided insights into the relevant racial politics that dominate Chicago both past and present.

Re-connections: Coast Salish Knitting and Resilience in Chicago (Canada) began as a conversation between Coast Salish knitters Adam Olsen and Joni Olsen, anthropologists Andrea Walsh and Trudi Lynn Smith, and historian Sylvia Olsen about the tensions between academic knowledge production and creative practices in Indigenous communities. During the residency, this conversation continued as the team used local archives and collections at the Field Museum to retrace the exhibition of Coast Salish knitting in the 1893 Columbian World's Fair. They used documentation of a ceremonial blanket performance staged at the 1893 monument entitled "A Signal for Peace" (C. Dallin, 1890) along with the historical data obtained from archival research to create new hand and machine knitted pieces in the gallery space (ET2013 Gallery Guide).

In addition to the works produced, the Coast Salish group held a demonstration and interactive knitting workshop at the Arts Incubator as mentioned earlier. The workshop was formed through a successful collaboration with Joanne Smith, organizer of a local group known as *Committed Knitters,* which holds regular "knit-ins" at the gallery through the support of the Arts Incubator and the local yarn shop, Loopy Yarns. This event brought in members of the community, primarily a community of knitters of various ages and cultural backgrounds, who shared their appreciation of knitting together with the Coast Salish group. The leaders of the workshop openly shared personal family anecdotes and photos, passed around knitted garments for participants to smell and feel, and established a sense of intimate, shared community.

Facing page, Sylvia and Adam Olsen, Chicago, 2013

The Coast Salish group pushed the boundaries of residency even further by a profound public demonstration of their work, which they also filmed. After collaborating with the Field Museum archivists to retrace the exhibition of Coast Salish knitting at the 1893 World's Fair, the group staged a contemporary ceremonial blanket performance in Garfield Park (near the Arts Incubator) on and around a replica statue of the original "Bulls with Maiden," which stood outside the Agricultural Building in the 1893 World's Fair. In effect, they reclaimed and re-appropriated the history of exhibition, creating new collaborative networks of meaning between past and present, communities and museums, insiders and outsiders. The Coast Salish group donated the blanket to the museum, creating a life for the "artwork" beyond the exhibition at the Arts Incubator and allowing it to find permanent residence in Chicago.

With *Shrines of Citizenship* (Portugal), the EBANO (Ethnography-Based Art Nomad Organization) Collective – comprised of artists and anthropologists Chiaro Pussetti, Victor Barros, and Lorenzo Bordonaro – produced a shrine as an interactive work reflecting upon citizenship and the inherent racial and nationalist politics. The EBANO Collective uses diverse art forms and media to explore the imaginaries ascribed to migration. Based upon several years of anthropological fieldwork with immigrant communities in Europe, their multimedia installation *Shrines of Citizenship* invited visitors to reflect upon the recent tightening of European migration policies, as well as the physical, bureaucratic, and symbolic barriers undocumented immigrants face around the world when pursuing the dream of citizenship. Their piece, a tall wooden bookshelf-like structure with off-white white wax heads sitting in water-filled jars on the shelves and illuminated from within. Water, wax, and other devotional objects, such as an enshrined passport, allude to the complexity of mobility and citizenship along all national borders, specifically evoking the memory of the thousands of people who disappeared in the Mediterranean Sea while attempting to reach Europe's southern border in the last decades, many of whom were from African countries (edited from Exhibition Brochure).

The EBANO Collective shared meaningful reflections about their experiences during the residency, meditating on their own boundary crossings—from Portugal to the U.S., and on a deeper level, the unanticipated challenges of

Facing page, EBANO's *Shrines of Citizenship*, Chicago, 2013

attempting to bring soil collected from Cape Verde to Europe and to the U.S., a movement interrupted by U.S. Customs. They commented on the additional compromises made to fit their work within the gallery space, given restrictions on using real candles and barbed wire. With work that focuses on boundary crossings through public art, these reflections provide an additional layer of meaning to the boundaries artists face in constructing their work within the frame of a gallery and a specific local context.

The EBANO Collective created the most memorable and critical contribution to the public roundtable event by entirely re-contextualizing their work during the event. Of all the artists, this collective was perhaps the most self-critical of their process, and of their inability to create a work that is interactive with its environment and community. During the roundtable, the collective dramatically turned their shrine around—from focusing inward towards gallery insiders to focusing out the windows to the local community. In this way, they were not only reflective but corrective. They mentioned that "being enclosed in gallery felt like a contradiction" to their larger public art practice and that they aimed to make an intervention in the public space. Here again, their inclusion in the residency program allowed for a conversation to emerge about sites of knowledge transmission and the role of a gallery in the community.

The final group to deal with "Cultural Immersions" was the artists, designers, and anthropologist who created a project called *Self-Repair* (Norway). The project was an extension of a residency in Norway at the Rogaland Art Center that investigated the notion of repair in terms of the relationship between that which is industrially manufactured and that which is produced through the touch of hands with needle and thread. For Chicago, this collective expands the notion of repair to research the topic of "self-repair" (eg. self-help, life coaching, positive thinking, aura-reading etc.) (ET2013 Gallery Guide). From their experiences undertaking such treatments in Chicago, they returned to the space of the residency to provide a creative "transcript" of their emotions during this fieldwork, a form of art therapy, transcribed onto a scroll of paper filled with creative reflections. It was readily apparent that the artists moved a project prepared and presented in Norway to this very unique and divergent local environment in Chicago. Nevertheless, it was in line with the experimental ambition of the residency in the Arts Incubator as their research in Chicago

explored similarities between anthropological and artistic methods in terms of participant-observation and subjective interpretations. During the residency they developed a pattern inspired and informed by this research specific to Chicago. The pattern was to be further developed after the residency, and the research from Chicago will form the basis for a Chicago line within the HAiK collection for Autumn/Winter 2014 (ET2013 Gallery Guide).
[FIGURE 14: Image 1938]

In Closing
Exhibition as Residency provided an invaluable window into an exhibition model that reveals the possibilities for collaborative artistic-anthropological exhibition within processes that push disciplinary discourses outside of conventional confines. However, the many ways in which boundaries were pushed defy a simple conclusion. Did *Exhibition as Residency* succeed in integrating themselves or fully taking residence in the neighborhood around them, that is, in breaking down some of the boundaries of race and class in South Chicago? Probably not. And, to be fair, this was outside the scope of what the exhibition aimed to do or what the artists possibly could achieve in the week of their residency. However, their visibly outsider presence in a Black neighborhood did offer a reflection on the role of projects such as this in breaking down the boundaries between artist insiders and audience outsiders through its larger commitment to create dialogue.

The *Exhibition as Residency* is best looked at as an experimental project that involved various interpretive communities and interpretive layers involving a diverse body of knowledge and a diverse community of stakeholders. In this cultural matrix, the artists, anthropologists, exhibition space, and local environment all work to co-produce anthropological knowledge and create cultural meaning. Perhaps the idealized goal of outsiders fully integrating into an unfamiliar community, given the constraints of the project, is overly ambitious. However, this exercise is critical to the future of exhibitionary practices. *Exhibition as Residency* took us on a journey that revealed just how important it is for exhibitions such as this to become a critical touchstone for conversations about the past, present, and future of art, anthropology, and insider/outsider exhibition practices.

Works Cited

Colapinto, John
2014 "The Real-Estate Artist: High-concept renewal on the South Side."
The New Yorker. January 20.

Ethnographic Terminalia
2013 Gallery Guide. Exhibition as Residency—Art, Anthropology,
Collaboration.

General installation view, Chicago, 2013

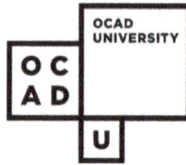

UNIVERSITY OF TORONTO

OCAD UNIVERSITY

UCIRVINE

CIVDDD

Social Sciences and Humanities Research Council of Canada

Conseil de recherches en sciences humaines du Canada

Canada

LUND UNIVERSITY
Joint Faculties of Humanities and Theology

Center for Basque Studies
UNIVERSITY OF NEVADA, RENO

College of Liberal Arts
University of Nevada, Reno

CALOUSTE GULBENKIAN FOUNDATION

EBANO COLLECTIVE

CHAPMAN UNIVERSITY

SIAT
SCHOOL OF INTERACTIVE ARTS + TECHNOLOGY

THE UNIVERSITY OF TEXAS AT AUSTIN

First Peoples' Heritage, Language & Culture Council

UCL

OCA
Office for Contemporary Art Norway

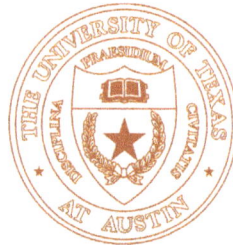

Sponsors and Supporters

Arts + Public Life (University of Chicago)
Society for Visual Anthropology
University College London (Department of Anthropology)
American Anthropological Association (The Community Engagement Fund)
University of Texas, Austin (Department of Anthropology)
Chapman University
School of Interactive Arts + Technology (Simon Fraser University)
Rachel Topham (Photographer)
Irine Prastio & Reese Muntean (Website)
Daniel Rudin (Videographer)
Amavong Panya (NFA Space, Chicago)
Elizabeth D'Antonio
Benjamin Haines
Forest Park Public Library
Harold Brown
Norman Teague
Mercedes Sahagun Zavala

Participants Supported by
OCA — Office for Contemporary Art Norway
Ontario College of Art and Design
University of Toronto
University of California, Irvine
Lunds University
Social Sciences and Humanities Research Council of Canada
Centre for Information Visualization and Date Driven Design established by the
Ontario Research Fund
EBANO Collective
University of Nevada, Reno (Center for Basque Studies | College of Liberal Arts)
Calouste Gulbenkian Foundation
First Peoples' Heritage, Language & Culture Council

ethnographic terminalia

exhibition as residency

ch
2

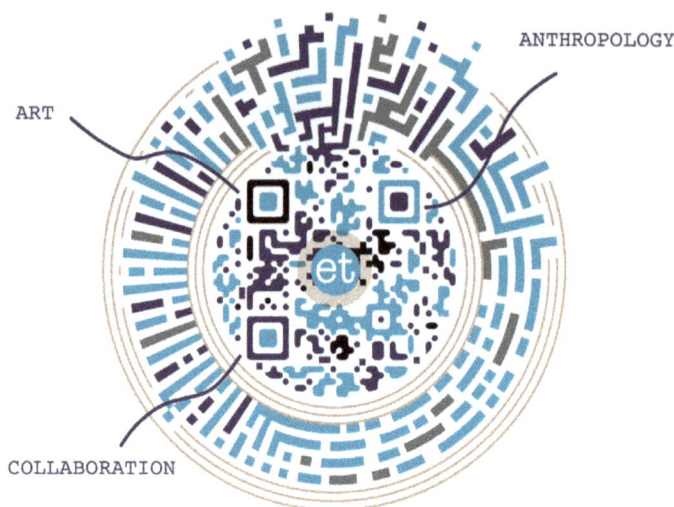

ANTHROPOLOGY

ART

et.

COLLABORATION

November 18 – 22, 2013

Arts Incubator in Washington Park

Second Floor Project Flex Space
301 E. Garfield Boulevard, Chicago, IL 60637

Exhibition Hours
M|W|TR: 12-3pm
F |: 12-6pm

Reception & Closing Ever
Friday November 22, 201:
6-9pm

Ethnographic Terminalia is an initiative that brings artists a anthropologists together to engage in emerging research through e

Exhibition as Residency is an installation of several international tive projects that visitors are invited to interact with in the galler; in exploring what lies within and beyond the disciplinary territor and anthropology, and how collaborations can shape new commur representations of cultural practice.

gallery encounter

Coast Salish Knitting

Sylvia Olsen, Adam Olsen, Joni Olsen, Andrea Walsh
& Trudi Smith

Date: Wednesday November 20, 2013
Time: 12:30-1:30pm

A public talk and demonstration by Coast Salish,
Tsartlip First Nation (Canada) knitters at the Arts
Incubator. This event brings communities
together to share and learn through fiber arts.
All welcome!

For more information visit:
www.ethnographicterminalia.org/2013galleryencounters

In Collaboration with:

SOUTHSIDE
economic
development
PROJECT

Arts+
Public
Life

First Peoples'
Heritage, Language &
Culture Council

CK
COMMITTED KNITTERS
— KNIT FOR TIME —

Loopy Yarns

ethnographic terminalia

exhibition as residency

ch
2

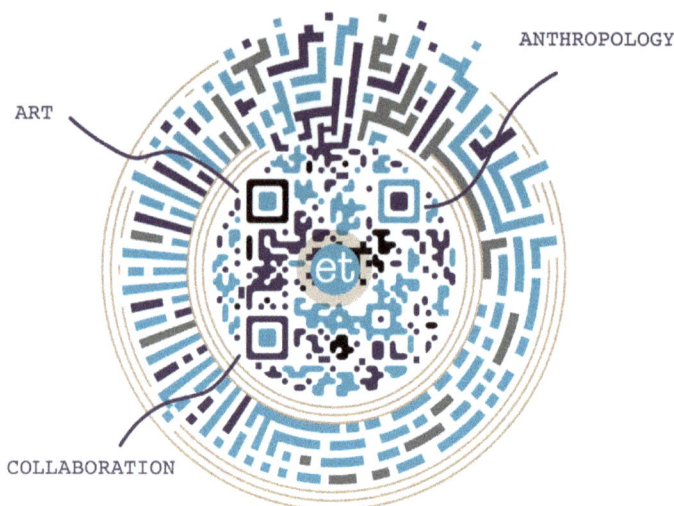

ART

ANTHROPOLOGY

et

COLLABORATION

November 18 - 22, 2013

Arts Incubator in Washington Park

Second Floor Project Flex Space
301 E. Garfield Boulevard, Chicago, IL 60637

Exhibition Hours
M|W|TR: 12-3pm
F |: 12-6pm

Reception & Closing Even
Friday November 22, 201
6-9pm

Ethnographic Terminalia is an initiative that brings artists
anthropologists together to engage in emerging research through e

Exhibition as Residency is an installation of several international
tive projects that visitors are invited to interact with in the galler
in exploring what lies within and beyond the disciplinary territor
and anthropology, and how collaborations can shape new commu
representations of cultural practice.

gallery encounter

Habitat with Ian Kirkpatrick

Dates:
Monday November 18, 2013
Wednesday November 19, 2013
Thursday November 20, 2013
 Friday November 21, 2013
Time: 12-3pm

Visit the Arts Incubator during public gallery hours to observe and talk with artist Ian Kirkpatrick as he works within his sculptural structure (a decorated container), as part if his critical reflection on the nature of museum objects and artefacts.

For more information visit:
www.ethnographicterminalia.org/2013galleryencounters

ethnographic terminalia
exhibition as residency

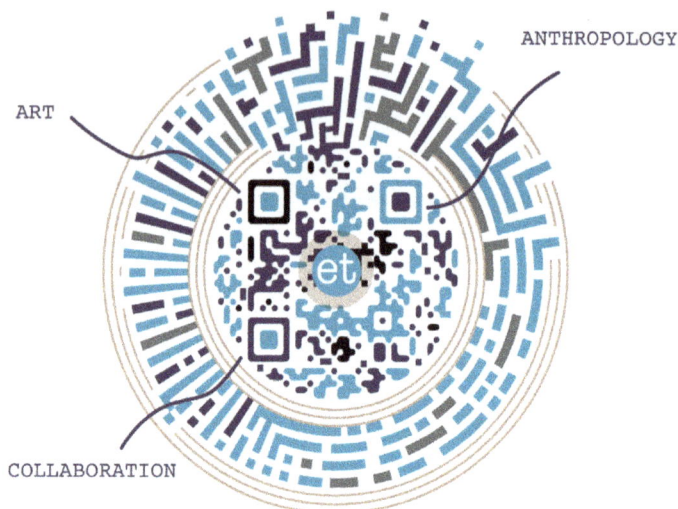

ANTHROPOLOGY

ART

COLLABORATION

November 18 – 22, 2013

Arts Incubator in Washington Park
Second Floor Project Flex Space
301 E. Garfield Boulevard, Chicago, IL 60637

Exhibition Hours
M|W|TR: 12-3pm
F |: 12-6pm

Reception & Closing Even
Friday November 22, 201:
6-9pm

Ethnographic Terminalia is an initiative that brings artists a
anthropologists together to engage in emerging research through e

Exhibition as Residency is an installation of several international
tive projects that visitors are invited to interact with in the galler
in exploring what lies within and beyond the disciplinary territor
and anthropology, and how collaborations can shape new commur
representations of cultural practice.

gallery encounter

Shrines of Citizenship
The EBANO Collective

Dates:
Monday November 18, 2013
Wednesday November 19, 2013
Thursday November 20, 2013
 Friday November 21, 2013
Time: 12-3pm

Come by during the Arts Incubator Public gallery hours to experience The EBANO Collective's interactive work—a shrine about citizenship where one must travel through obstacles (real and imagined) to explore and learn more about issues of migration and identity.

For more information visit:
www.ethnographicterminalia.org/2013galleryencounters

Supported by:

EBANO
COLLECTIVE

ethnographic terminalia

exhibition as residency

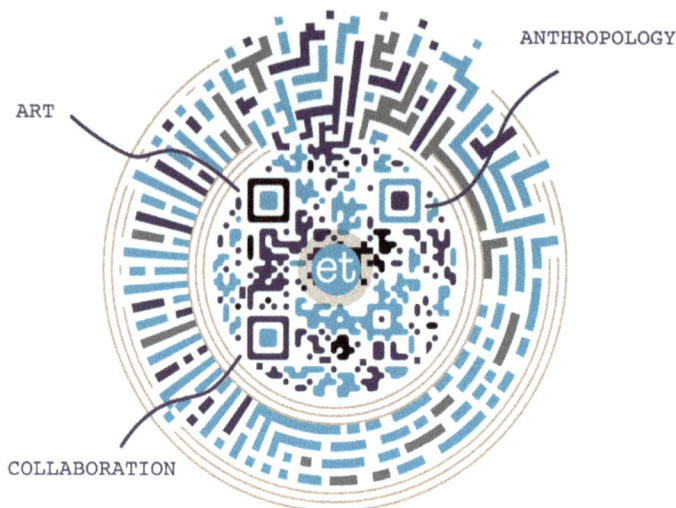

ANTHROPOLOGY

ART

COLLABORATION

et.

November 18 – 22, 2013

Arts Incubator in Washington Park

Second Floor Project Flex Space
301 E. Garfield Boulevard, Chicago, IL 60637

Exhibition Hours
M|W|TR: 12-3pm
F |: 12-6pm

Reception & Closing Even
Friday November 22, 201
6-9pm

Ethnographic Terminalia is an initiative that brings artists a
anthropologists together to engage in emerging research through e

Exhibition as Residency is an installation of several international c
tive projects that visitors are invited to interact with in the gallery
in exploring what lies within and beyond the disciplinary territor
and anthropology, and how collaborations can shape new commun
representations of cultural practice.

gallery encounter

Visualizing Place through Art & Anthropology

Date: Thursday November 21, 2013
Time: 2-3pm

Join Robert Willim (anthropologist), Jesse Colin Jackson (artist), Tori Foster (artist), & Lindsay A. Bell (anthropologist) as they share through an open discussion and interactive engagement how they experiment with visualizing communities in the Washington Park area through film and digital media.

For more information visit:
www.ethnographicterminalia.org/2013galleryencounters

Supported By:

LUNDS UNIVERSITET
Humanistiska och teologiska fakulteterna

OCAD UNIVERSITY
OCAD U

UCIRVINE

UNIVERSITY OF TORONTO

CIVDDD
Centre for Innovation in Information Visualization and Data Driven Design

Social Sciences and Humanities
Research Council of Canada

Conseil de recherches en
sciences humaines du Canada

Canadá

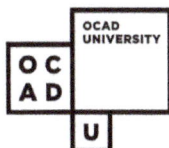

ethnographic terminalia
exhibition as residency

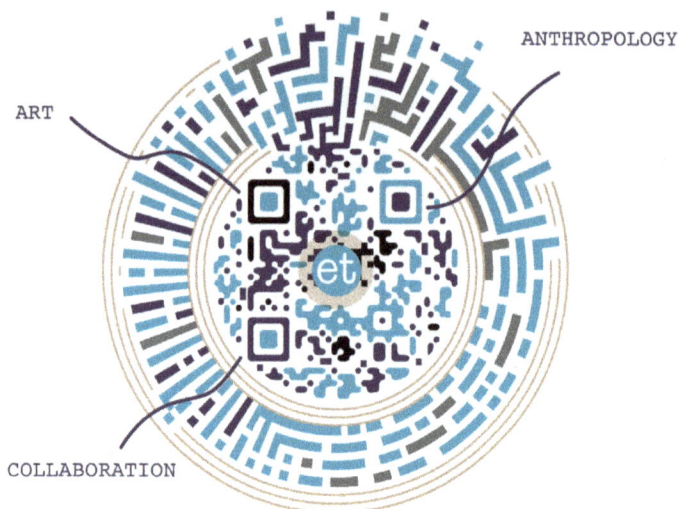

ch
2

ANTHROPOLOGY

ART

COLLABORATION

November 18 – 22, 2013

Arts Incubator in Washington Park
Second Floor Project Flex Space
301 E. Garfield Boulevard, Chicago, IL 60637

Exhibition Hours
M|W|TR: 12-3pm
F |: 12-6pm

Reception & Closing Eve:
Friday November 22, 201
6-9pm

Ethnographic Terminalia is an initiative that brings artists
anthropologists together to engage in emerging research through

Exhibition as Residency is an installation of several international
tive projects that visitors are invited to interact with in the galler
in exploring what lies within and beyond the disciplinary territor
and anthropology, and how collaborations can shape new commu
representations of cultural practice.

gallery encounter

The Ethnographic Process of Portrait-Painting with Zoe Bray

Dates:
Monday November 18, 2013
Wednesday November 19, 2013
Thursday November 20, 2013
 Friday November 21, 2013
Time: 12-3pm

Every 20mins, the artist will break from painting a model in the gallery during public hours to talk with visitors about her unique ethnographic process that involves naturalist/realist painting.

For more information visit:
www.ethnographicterminalia.org/2013galleryencounters

Supported By:

Center for
Basque Studies
UNIVERSITY OF NEVADA, RENO

College of Liberal Arts
University of Nevada, Reno